granny chic

First published in Great Britain in 2012
by Kyle Books, an imprint of Kyle Cathie Ltd
23 Howland Street, London W1T 4AY
general.enquiries@kylebooks.com
www.kylebooks.com

10 9 8 7 6 5 4 3 2 1

ISBN 978-0-85783-155-2

Editor: Judith Hannam
Editorial assistant: Tara O'Sullivan
Copy editor: Anna Hitchin
Designer: Helen Bratby
Stylists: Tif Fussell & Rachelle Blondel
Photographer: Catherine Gratwicke
Production: Lisa Pinnell

A Cataloguing in Publication record for this
title is available from the British Library.

Colour reproduction by Alta Image
Printed and bound in China by C & C Offset Ltd

* except photographs on pp18, 31, 65, 103, 108, 111 © Tif Fussell

granny chic

Crafty recipes & inspiration for the handmade home

Tif Fussell & Rachelle Blondel

Photography by Catherine Gratwicke

Kyle Books

contents

117
more crafty recipes to fill your heart with glee

****

159
terribly interesting things for your crafty soul to know

****

Tif Fussell

Tif Fussell is a Brit living stateside in an odd-looking mock tudor house called Mossy Shed, along with her clan and various critters. She spends her days wisely with her trusty sewing machine, Miss Ethel, and pottling the aisles of her local thrift store. Proud to be a self-taught crafter, on any given day she can be found rambling upon her blog www.dottieangel. blogspot.com and selling her handcrafted wares in her store www.dottieangel.etsy. com. Tif is the author of best-selling indie book *dottie angel – the peachy crafty life of Tif Fussell*, published by Uppercase, and is currently teaching workshops stateside and in the UK. She likes to dabble with a little thing called 'her imagination' whilst dressed in her best granny chic finery and is quite convinced everyone has a crafty soul inside waiting to be polished.

Rachelle Blondel

Rachelle Blondel lives in a ramshackle farmhouse in the Yorkshire Dales with her family, an array of various critters and a huge collection of what-not... Her adventures are written down for all to see on her blog www.talesoftedandagnes. blogspot.com. She is a dabbler and believes that anything can be made from nothing – it just takes a crafty eye, a needle and thread plus a few old bits and bobs... By day she makes accessories for people and their homes, using the most British of materials, then sells them in various boutiques and online at www. tedandagnes.co.uk. Rachelle also likes to run the odd workshop or two and spread the word far and wide about the wonderful world of granny chic.

Tif and Rachelle are most happy to be treading the righteous and goodly path of handcrafted and secondhand. They nurture their crafty souls daily, whilst wearing rose-coloured specs and surrounding themselves with granny chic goodness.

Rachelle's workspace

Tif's workspace

'do embrace all that is granny chic
and give it a forever home'

hello dearest readers,

We are most delighted to have you pick up our crafty book and give it a gander. As you flick through the pages we would like to introduce you to our handcrafted secondhand homes and show you how to make a thing or two of your own.

So if you too have a fondness for vintage fabrics, yarny goodness and forgotten finds with a tale to tell, then this book will be your cup of tea. Jammy packed with things to make and ideas to glean, alongside rambling notes on this and that, it will have you reaching for your rose-coloured specs, rustling in your vintage fabric stash (or indeed starting one) and digging deep to find your inner granny chic crafting soul. For we do love a peachy bit of vintage fabric, doily or thrifted find! Being inspired by our own grandmothers' stitching, knitting and crocheting was a huge influence on us both and we grew up to embrace all that is goodly and righteous.

The giddy feeling of finding a vintage fabric or an old piece of furniture and dragging it home never ever goes away. It is the anticipation of the find, the 'not knowing what forsaken soul you will come across in your thrifty trip', which has us addicted. We think it's quite true to say that our way of decorating a home can be perfectly summed up with the name 'granny chic'.

However, a word of caution before we proceed… It is quite possible upon reading this book that you will in turn become addicted to the ways of handmade and secondhand living inspired by grannies in days gone by. Or possibly you already are, and this would not surprise us, for there are many such as ourselves already living such a life. Either way, when the need to create a handmade home gets into your crafty soul, there is no going back… Getting your daily fix or thrill from stitching up a cushion, painting an old chair or patching together a curtain is a grand way to spend the day we believe.

Hurrah hooray! Then let us begin…

Rachelle and Tif

stay a while

dottie angel

Classic

29c

crafty
ways
bring
sunny
days

TED
&
AGNES

handmade accessories
& vintage whatnot

THE THREE BEARS

dottie
angel

a 'perfectly peachy' half pinny

Dearest readers,

The moment I pop on a pinny, be it a half or a full one,
I am transported to a time when it was perfectly normal to
wear a pinny as your daily attire. I may be having to do rather
dull chores, such as laundry, sweeping or indeed the evening
meal (not my forte), but this is made so much peachier
when I am wearing a pinny in pretty prints and vintage lace...
This little recipe I have to share has endless possibilities as to
how you may choose to adorn it: be it with a doily, a patchwork
pocket or a snippet or two of lace, it is entirely up to you! Tif x

ingredients

* one used tea towel from the
  kitchen drawer, washed & ironed
* one napkin or placemat
* some odd lengths of vintage lace
* several hemmed edges cut from
  old vintage sheets or some twill tape
* your handy dandy sewing kit
* a trusty sewing machine

crafty ways bring sunny days

With right sides facing up, lay your tea towel flat and with the napkin a-top, placed slightly left of the centre of the tea towel. Pin in place and stitch around three sides with your trusty sewing machine. Be sure to leave the top edge unstitched thus transforming your napkin into a handy dandy pocket.

Along the bottom edge of your pinny (i.e. tea towel) stitch some lace. You could use one whole length of lace or indeed odd bits to give it a nice 'hodge podge' effect.

Next, taking long strips of the hemmed edges cut from old sheets, make the straps. Fold under the raw short ends, press and then pin to the two top corners of the wrong side of your pinny and stitch down. To avoid frayed edges at the other end of your straps, fold, press and stitch them. By all means, you may also wish to use twill tape instead (and proceed as directed above) if you do not wish to cut into your vintage sheets stash, I totally understand.

Put on a pretty frock and clogs, wrap your granny chic pinny around your waist and immediately feel peachier about your daily chores.

Just a note:

I am also thinking it might be nice to add some hand-embroidered wording on the pocket before you stitch it down. Just a thought worth pondering. I am partial to 'high hopes'; always good to have a pocket full of high hopes in my opinion!

Always be prepared for any situation where your hands may be idle. Have a little stitching or crochet stashed in your bag, so you can whip it out at any given moment. Be warned, this can often trigger eye-rolling or other such behaviour from your nearest and dearest as you create more wonders for your abode. However, it can also lead to many passing folks striking up a lovely conversation along the lines of "Goodness me! My granny used to crochet" and a trip down memory lane is sure to follow.

glorious gladys

a perfectly round cushion

Dearest readers,

In my opinion there is nothing nicer than a perfectly round cushion. They are suited to all sorts of locations around your abode but are especially at home on top of a freshly painted stool. Now this recipe is one that originally began as a much smaller lavender pillow designed for my first sewing exam at the young age of 12. So with a bit of tweaking and twiddling this larger version works a treat, in fact I guarantee once you have made one you will be quite smitten with everything that is round & cushiony like. *Rachelle x*

ingredients

* a large piece of paper
* a round cushion pad
* scraps of fabric
* a square of base fabric
* 2 spiffy buttons big enough to cover the centre gathering of your cushion
* your handy dandy sewing kit

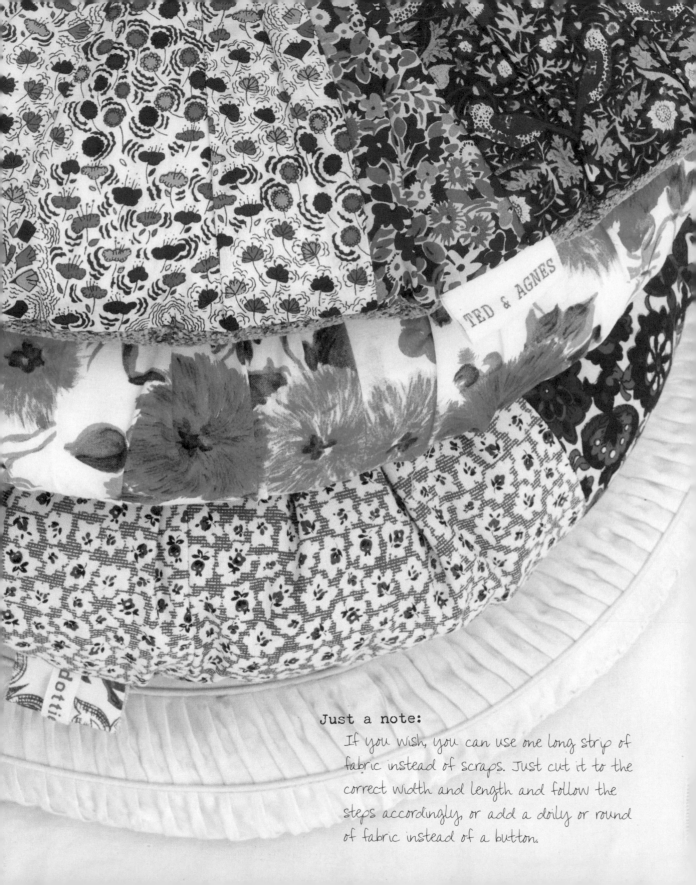

Just a note:
If you wish, you can use one long strip of fabric instead of scraps. Just cut it to the correct width and length and follow the steps accordingly, or add a doily or round of fabric instead of a button.

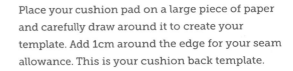
Place your cushion pad on a large piece of paper and carefully draw around it to create your template. Add 1cm around the edge for your seam allowance. This is your cushion back template.

Measure around the outside edge of your cushion pad and add 2cm for seam allowance. This is the length of your fabric scraps. Divide the diameter (measure across the centre from edge to edge) in half and add 1cm. This is the width of your fabric scraps.

Place your cushion back template onto your base fabric and cut around it.

Cut your fabric scraps to the correct width and then stitch up your scraps into a long strip, making sure they are the correct length. Press all the seams flat.

Stitch the short ends of the strip together to create a tube and press the seam. Pin a long edge of the strip around the edge of the base fabric. You may also wish to tack the fabric at this stage. Stitch around the edge, clip the seams and press.

Turn your cushion cover to the right side and lay your pad onto the wrong side of the base. Taking a double length of strong thread, sew small stiches along the top of the fabric, gathering your stitches as you go.

Gather all the stitches up tightly and secure. Thread a button onto the needle and stitch through to the centre of the back of the cushion.

Pull the thread tight and then secure. Cover these stitches with another button, doily or something else that takes your fancy, smooth out the fabric and place somewhere for all to admire...

patched fabric

Patching and piecing old fabrics, vintage white-work and embroidered table runners together is a peachy way of using materials that perhaps are a little the worse for wear and in their current state would not be usable. When out and about on your thrifty pottling, always be on the lookout for vendors with baskets and containers overflowing with big old messy heaps of doilies, lace and vintage linens. These are usually the places you can pick up wonderful old cloth treasures for very little money because of the tears and stains that make them less worthy in other folks' eyes.

But to us, the ones with granny chic souls, these sad forgotten pieces are 'oh so worthy' of bringing home and washing through and pondering how we can make them shine again.

It is perfectly normal, when upon discovery of such linen lovelies, to have a moment when your heart pitter patters a little faster and you feel your eyes welling up with tears of joy. You may look around and wonder why no other thrifty soul appears to have noted what you have seen. Do not allow that to make you doubt what your rose-coloured specs have shown you. No sirree! Even if your lovely finds may have seen better days and others are oblivious to their potential, believe in your crafty instinct and listen to its little voice.

When returning home victorious, it is very lovely to share your spoils with clan members, critters included. Expect mixed reactions, as not all clan members have rose-coloured specs. Critters, however, are on the whole born with them, so they are usually your best advocates since when others roll their eyes heavenwards and exclaim at the crappity crap they see, you and the critters see only peachiness. Now would be a good time to wash your finds carefully, making sure not to put them under any more stress than they have already been through in their lost state. After which, it is nice to treat them well, taking time to pop them in the right pile with their like-minded friends, that way when you are working on your next project and require a table runner perhaps, you will know exactly where to find your lovely collection. Take pride in displaying your linen lovelies; have

them on view atop retro cabinets or behind the glass doors of a granny chic dresser. When inspiration strikes they will be there waiting patiently for you, ready for you to rummage through them and find the exact little something to start you on your merry crafty way.

We are fond of the good old-fashioned habit of draping a lace runner over a sideboard, or using a tablecloth to do a lovely job of covering up a less than pretty table still waiting for its moment to be transformed. But before you dismiss this as being rather 'fuddy duddy', we beg you to reconsider. Several different tray cloths with pretty colourful embroidery and stunning crocheted edging, cut and layered in such a manner as to highlight their good points and hide their flaws, can make a très modern granny chic attire for your mantelpiece. Add a few knick knacks from your growing collection of thrifty souls, a vase of kitschy faux flowers and perhaps a mirror or two, and you will have a unique fireplace with a vintage vibe.

Patching and piecing together linens can be done quite easily in two ways. The first one is to slowly build up your layers and every time you add a new piece, pin it and stitch it with the aid of your trusty sewing machine. You can use self-coloured thread or choose a contrasting jolly colour. The second way is to layer all your pieces in one go, carefully pin through all your

materials and then with a needle and embroidery thread, go about stitching everything down. You can use the opportunity to add a few embroidery stitches of your own or you could do some simple running stitch.

Think about changing colour threads, making nice little frayed knots to start off the piece and even leaving some happy tails of thread after you have finished.

Sometimes you may need to ponder things before you cut into your linen pieces. If this is the case and you have Mr Doubter upon your shoulder, we suggest you perhaps pop your pinned piece in the place it is intended for, add a few knick knacks and then walk away. As you pass through the area for the next day or so, your crafty heart will tell you if it looks peachy or pants.

Once you have the hang of chopping up your fabric finds and patching them back together, you can branch out to find other areas of your granny chic abode to decorate in this style.

We often find ourselves using patched and pieced fabrics for window panels and for curtains across the front of bookcases or perhaps stapled inside glass cupboard doors. Cushion covers,

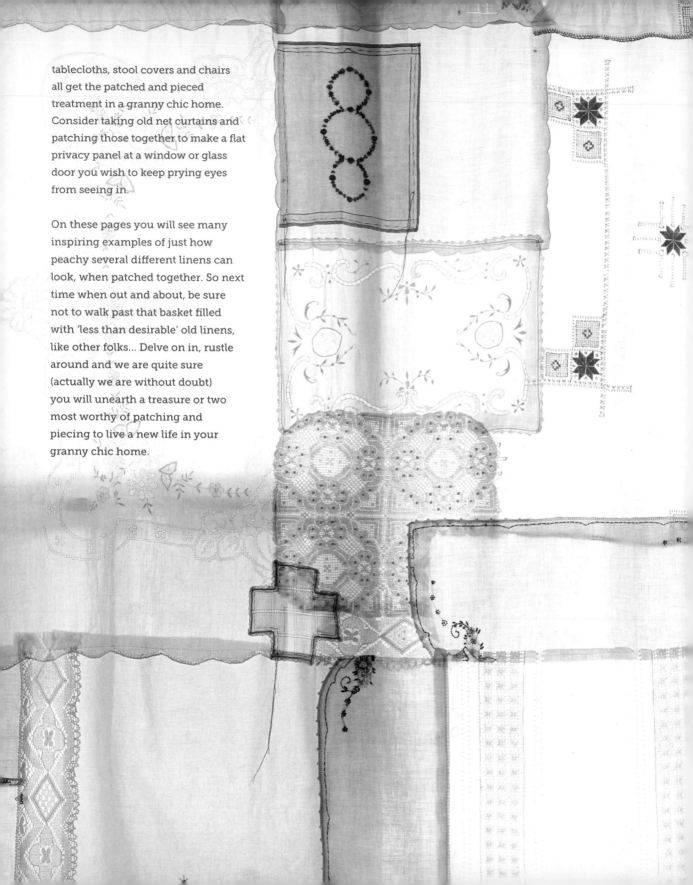

tablecloths, stool covers and chairs all get the patched and pieced treatment in a granny chic home. Consider taking old net curtains and patching those together to make a flat privacy panel at a window or glass door you wish to keep prying eyes from seeing in.

On these pages you will see many inspiring examples of just how peachy several different linens can look, when patched together. So next time when out and about, be sure not to walk past that basket filled with 'less than desirable' old linens, like other folks... Delve on in, rustle around and we are quite sure (actually we are without doubt) you will unearth a treasure or two most worthy of patching and piecing to live a new life in your granny chic home.

With all this wonderful fabric about your abode, the need for a sewing kit close at hand is essential. Keep all your bits and bobs in a tin, jar or some other suitable what-not, and make sure when you have used them, you put them straight back. Things to include are needles, threads of various colours and strengths, scissors, tape measure, seam ripper, tape, tailors' chalk, pins, elastic, embroidery thread, fabric glue and anything else that could possibly be useful at some point or other.

When these cloths are on their last legs move them on to floor cloth status or maybe for cleaning the car...

make-do dishcloths

Dearest readers,

After having a jolly good sort out of the linen cupboard, I came across a pile of forgotten, worn-out flannels. No longer lovely enough to wash one's face but too good to throw away, so I hatched a plan. I use cloths in the kitchen for all manner of jobs and like to have a pile of them waiting in the wings. So adding a little binding gives them the chance to be loved again. *Rachelle X*

ingredients

* old washcloths/flannels or old towels
* pretty bias binding
* your handy dandy sewing kit

recipe

Give your washcloths or towel a quick iron and then cut the towel into usable squares or cut away the bulky hems from the sides of the washcloths.

Measure around each washcloth and add 2cm and then cut this length of bias binding. If your bias binding needs to be folded, do so now and give it a good old press.

With the end of the binding start 1cm in from one of the corners on your washcloth and pin the binding all around the edge of the cloth. When you reach the raw edge, slightly overlap the binding and pin.

Stitch around the edge, going through all three layers of binding, cloth and binding, and then press.

crafty ways bring sunny days

a most sensible fabric rug

Dearest readers,

One morning I awoke with the notion that I would indeed pull up the wood effect lino that furnished our kitchen and hallway floors and paint them a delightful manor house grey... Yes, there was a touch of insanity there but as happy as I am with the result, I needed a little something to break up the colour and protect the floor from certain members of the household who are unable to use the door mat... So, unable to find a suitable rug, I decided to make this rather hardwearing fabric one that would indeed have taken pride of place in our grannies' hallways. Rachelle x

ingredients

* non-slip rug backing
* a sturdy piece of fabric or pieces of fabric patched together
* fabric glue
* fabric scraps and doilies, lacy bits or other embellishments that catch your eye
* fancy coloured thread
* matt varnish
* your handy dandy sewing kit

Measure the exact size that you would like your rug to be and cut this size out of the non-slip rug backing.

Using this as a template, lay it onto the wrong side of your chosen fabric and draw around the non-slip backing. Mark a 5cm border around it. This is your cutting line. Cut out the fabric, following the line, then remove the non-slip rug backing template.

Fold over the 5cm border, as if making a hem, and press well so that you have a sharp edge. Glue the border down, making sure you get plenty of glue on the edge to prevent the fabric fraying. Leave to dry completely.

Turn to right side, then glue or stitch on patches of fabric, fancy stitches, a doily or whatever takes your fancy.

When you are happy with your rug, paint it with the first coat of varnish, working it well into the fabric. Leave to dry.

Turn the rug over and varnish the underside. This gives the rug a little more protection and stability.

Repeat the last two steps at least four times, or more if you would like a very long-lasting and well-wearing rug.

Once the rug is completely dry, tack the prepared non-slip rug fabric to its underside and lay it on the floor. Admire, keeping a close eye out for any wayward animals who may feel it's a suitable place to rest!

Just a note:

Keep your rug clean with a quick lick of the mop and swift sweep of the brush. No soaking or washing...that just wouldn't do....

There are spaces in your home that lend themselves to being calm and uncluttered.... hallways and spaces between are great examples of where you can display just one stunning piece such as a lampshade or a wall hanging and really give it room to shine.

crafty ways bring sunny days

✳ Vintage and retro bed sheets often have the most marvellous floral patterns and colours of the sort not seen nowadays. Check for wear and tear and, if all is well, nab them up with a gleeful twinkle in your eye and bring them home for a good old whirl in the machine. You may not know at the time what you will use them for, but a cupboard full of freshly laundered old sheets is a sight to behold and one surely to inspire.

✳ The possibilities their 'lightweight yardage of little cost' can offer are endless… from chopping in half and hanging at the window, to cutting up to make nighties. Or take several of your fave sheets, cut them into strips and sew them back together, giving a striped patchwork effect, perfect for laying across folding tables at parties. Even sheets in the sorriest of threadbare states can be made into dusters.

a patched & pieced lampshade

Dearest readers,
In our family room we do not have ceiling lights and as you can imagine this makes reading très tricky, so I have become most fond of adding table lamps as and where I can. On occasion I will hang a lampshade using a light fitting and cable set, dingly-dangling from a handy dandy hook in the ceiling. This recipe is perfect for using up odd scraps of lace and table runners which have seen better days and old lamp frames you come across on your thrifty travels. There is no right or wrong way to patch and piece them together – just enjoy the process and when it is all over, be sure to step back and note a perfectly peachy lampshade shedding a little light in your life, be it hanging from a handy dandy hook in the ceiling or indeed outside amongst other 'framed friends'. Tif x

ingredients

✵ a thrift store lampshade
✵ pieces of old lace tablecloths
✵ a vintage embroidered table runner
✵ embroidery thread in happy colours
✵ your handy dandy sewing kit
✵ a light fitting and cable set

crafty ways bring sunny days

First things first: you must strip the fabric off your lampshade, doing it with some care so as not to damage the frame. You should be left with a metal frame clear of all fabric and all glue by the time you have finished.

Cut several pieces from your old lace cloth and start to lay them vertically across the open gaps of your frame. You may need to hold up one or two pieces to check the sizing is correct before you start to snippety snip. Be sure to overlap your pieces of fabric along the top and bottom rims of the frame. If some pieces are not quite long enough, you can stitch them together prior to attaching them to the frame.

When you are happy with the placement of your first few lace cloth pieces, hold them together with pins to keep them in place. Then, with needle and embroidery thread, hand stitch the panels together, making sure they stay nice and taut against the frame. You could use running stitch or cross stitch, and might like to change your colour threads every now and then.

You should intersperse the lace panels with pieces cut from the vintage embroidered table runner – this will allow you to see through certain areas of the lampshade and not through others.

Slowly but surely, work your way around the frame, stitching the panels together. Be sure to make a few stitches around the metal rims at the top and bottom, to keep the fabric in place.

When you have covered your whole frame with patched cloth and sewn it in place, attach a light cord set and hang it from a hook with an energy bulb. (If this is a little tricky to do, then read the instructions that came with your light cord set and attach as suggested by the nice folks at the manufacturing company of light cord sets). Switch on, step back and see how lovely the light looks peeking through the lace panels and casting a rosy glow around your abode.

Just a note:

If you wish, you can wrap your metal frame with fabric or lace before you start stitching the panels of fabric on. I did not as I rather liked the contrast of the pretty vintage lace work with the raw metal frame, however you may not.

crafty ways bring sunny days

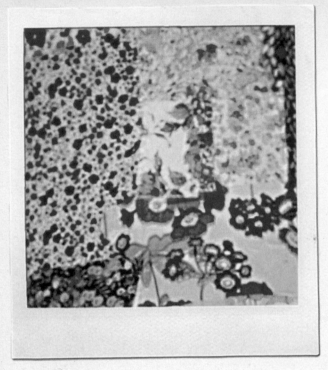

Now lampshades of all shapes and sizes are a must for any granny chic home but some are often a little worse for wear and a quick fix is needed. Give them a quick dust and remove or fix any trims or edging. Use the method on page 56 for the wrapped up chair to give your lampshades a new lease of life casting a warm glow around your abode...

crafty ways bring sunny days

Fabrics suited to a
granny chic home are
varied. It is all about
what makes your heart skip.
Large floral blooms upon vintage
linen are most lovely indeed,
and do not dismiss ditsy teeny tiny
florals, for these can make splendid
scraps for patching or indeed, yarn
fabric balls. Bark cloth fabric is a
tried and true granny fabric and mighty
fine examples can still be found on
eBay, in vintage stores and
whilst browsing.

all wrapped up chair

Dearest readers, well, there isn't a day goes past when I don't look at my scraps pile and wonder at what I can wrap them around next. The table legs, my fridge, the lampshades and even my caravan have not escaped my slight obsession with glue and fabric.
But my favourite has to be the simple but perfectly lovely wrapped chair. Rachelle x

ingredients

* a wooden chair
* sandpaper, sponge, brushes
* wallpaper paste or watered down PVA glue
* fabric scraps
* a craft knife
* matt varnish

recipe

First things first: give your chair a jolly good scrub with hot soapy water to remove any dirt, residue or rogue pieces of gum that may be lurking on it. Once it is thoroughly dry, sand your chair until it feels smooth. Wipe it over with a damp cloth.

Next, mix up your wallpaper paste in a large bowl as instructed on the packet, or thin down your PVA about 50:50 with water. Stir really well and place to one side. If you keep your glue or paste covered, it will be usable for several days.

Whilst your chair is drying, sort out your pile of fabric scraps so they are close at hand, cutting away any wayward threads or wonky bits.

Place some pieces of fabric to soak in the bowl of glue. Then decide on a small area of the chair where you want to begin wrapping, and paint some glue onto it.

Take a piece of fabric from the bowl and place it onto the patch of glue on the chair, smoothing it out using your fingers, the glue brush or a damp sponge.

Keep wrapping, patching and smoothing until you have covered your chair. Then, using the brush, paint a layer of glue over the fabric, really working it into your patches.

Let this dry completely and then give the chair several coats of varnish, letting it dry completely between coats.

At this point, let your eyes wander around your abode and imagine what else you could indeed wrap in fabric...

Just a note:

To get the best results from this project it is necessary to get messy, so make sure you are not wearing your best outfit. A pinny is essential.

crafty ways bring sunny days

Often you fall in love, part with precious pennies and cart home a piece of furniture whose wrappings are not really to your liking. Give it a good clean and then raid your scraps pile for suitable bits of fabric. Armed with your handy dandy sewing kit and staple gun, pin fabric onto the piece and then cut around leaving 1cm extra to turn and stitch or staple. Try to follow the seam lines of the original cover as this will help you ease the fabric to fit. Patch and piece to your heart's delight and enjoy. Remember, if you get fed up with the fabric, whip it all off and start again!

crafty ways bring sunny days

the ever-useful scraps of fabric

A heap of fabric scraps, along with a handy dandy sewing kit is an absolute must in any crafty home. We both sport a rather large fabric hoard, from metres of prized vintage cloth to tiny bits kept lovingly 'just in case'. Unfortunately, with such an addiction a rather large scrap bag is par for the course, along with the constant thoughts of what all the bits and pieces might possibly be used for. Fabric should always be on the top of your list when trawling the charity shops, wandering the boot fair fields, jumble and yard sales. Don't dismiss anything that catches your eye, for there is always some use for even the tiniest scrap of fabric.

Several projects in this book show you the way to use some of your scraps up, and we have listed a few more here.

Knotted fabric yarn
Super for wrapping around handles, lampshades, chairs, bicycles, table legs and anything that stands still longer than a moment. Just tear thin strips of fabric, knot them together and roll the resulting string up into a super looking ball, ready to jump to it when needs must.

Stitched together strips
Stitching odd strips of fabric together to make a piece of usable fabric will make a great cushion cover, bag or wall hanging, to name but a few. The selvedge of a vintage fabric is always rather special stitched in this way, and let's face it, it's not really much use for anything else...

Patchwork
Not a new notion it's true, but by using glue instead of thread a whole new world comes to light... With this method there is nothing safe from a wee bit of patching. If you want it to be waterproof too, team it up with a suitable varnish.

A staple gun can become your best friend in no time at all. Be sure to keep stocked up on staples for you never know when a fabby piece of fabric will find you and you'll be rushing home to spend five quality minutes making a kitchen chair look très peachy with nothing more than your new fabric find, your handy dandy staple gun and a cup of tea by your side.

a 'happy heart' kantha cushion

Dearest readers,

Nothing says granny chic more than a settee piled high with floral fabric cushions. A lovely mismatch of patterns and granny coloured fabrics, inviting passers-by to rest a while. Envelope back cushion-covers are by far the easiest way of making covers, I believe, and if you make them out of one long piece of patched fabric, even more so. In this recipe we will dabble with a traditional form of stitching called kantha to produce a quilted 'happy heart' for appliquéing on the cushion cover. I have split the recipe into two parts for easy understanding. In the first bit I'll explain how we make our little kantha heart and then the second bit shows you how to make the cushion cover and attach your lovely happy heart. Tif x

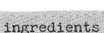 **ingredients**

✳ an old bit of wallpaper for cutting out
   the heart template
✳ a lovely mix of cotton fabrics, vintage or new
   'vintage inspired' ones if you like
✳ a trusty iron and board
✳ pins and scissors
✳ a piece of paper and pencil for scribbling notes
   if need be (or use the margin of this page)
✳ a square cushion insert of the size you wish to make
✳ a trusty sewing machine and thread
✳ a sharp needle
✳ thin cotton thread (the sort used for crocheting doilies)

crafty ways bring sunny days

Making the kantha heart

The size of your cushion determines how big your kantha heart will be. Therefore, as a rough guide, make sure your finished heart will have an area around it at least 5cm from the cushion edge. With this knowledge, you can go ahead and draw out a heart on your old wallpaper. Do not fret about making it perfectly perfect, far better to have one that is slightly uneven than too round and symmetrical.

Cut out your wallpaper heart pattern and then place it upon three layers of old lightweight fabrics (like bedsheeting). Pin it down and then cut around it (this will be your padding between the top layer and the cushion cover).

Next, patch together three different fabrics of your choice, large enough to place your heart pattern on. Carefully cut around the pattern but this time be sure to leave a 1.5cm seam allowance all the way around the paper heart as you cut out your fabric.

With the right side of patched fabric heart facing down, place the three inner layers on top. Carefully, with an iron, turn and press the outer edge of the patched heart over the inner layers. You may have to make a few snips to get around the corners.

When you have pressed it all around, turn it over and you will have a lightly padded fabric heart with edges turned under, ready to be kantha stitched on top of your cushion fabric. For now, place the heart to one side.

Putting it all together

Measure your cushion insert. To make the cover, you will need a piece of fabric which measures the same height as your pillow, (plus 2.5cm for seam allowance) and then slightly more than two and a half times the width of your pillow. Write down your measurements lest you forget. This is where you can just cut one large piece of fabric if you do not wish to have a patched cushion, or gather together a few of your favourite fabrics and start cutting strips of different widths and stitch them together. Be sure to press the seams nicely.

When you have made the correct sized rectangle of fabric for your cushion insert, take your prepared patched heart piece and lay it in the middle of the rectangle, right sides facing up. Pin it in place, making sure the seams are turned under.

With a needle and cotton thread, slip stitch around the outline of the heart. Then, beginning at the bottom of the heart, slowly sew tiny running stitches in rows along the heart, going back and forth, keeping close together. As you work up the heart in this manner you will see the fabric being quilted together. When you get to the top, finish off on the reverse side neatly.

Now you are ready to make up the cushion cover. Press and fold the seams for the two short ends of your patched rectangle of fabric and pin in place. Stitch in place with your trusty sewing machine.

Lay your rectangle of fabric right side facing up. Take one end and fold towards the centre of your rectangle, going past the centre point. Then do the same for the other end, overlapping in the middle. With a tape measure, you will need to check you have the exact width of your pillow insert. If it is too small or too wide, then readjust your fabric accordingly.

When happy with the width, pin in place along the top and bottom raw edges and stitch, leaving a 1.25cm seam allowance. You may wish to go back over the raw edges with zig zag stitch, but you do not have to.

Carefully snip your corners before turning right sides out, and press. Place your cushion insert in your 'happy heart' kantha pillow-cover and do a bit of plumping before finding a most fitting spot for it to feel at home.

You could make this recipe even more easy peasy by using one fabric, literally cut to shape, stitching up two sides and voilà! A simple happy cushion.

Some frocks are far too peachy to hide away. Consider, instead, wrapping a handy dandy clothes rail in fabric and hanging your favourite frocks from vintage hangers, for all to admire.

In this space every piece of furniture, some in view (and others sneakily hiding from you), started life in different decades. This is a perfect example of how a mish-mash of styles, when all placed together, become one big happy family, thus highlighting the wonder of granny chic and its embracing ways.

See this book as a guidebook, one to come back to time and again. Perhaps make your own notes in the margin, stick in note pages and colour swatches to refer back to. A scrapbook of granny chic, what inspires you. Make lists of what you are looking out for when out and about, but bear in mind, sometimes it's the unexpected finds that are the most thrilling. You may not have known you needed a certain peachy find until you stumble across it and realise it is the perfect finishing touch to a vignette you have been working on.

crafty ways bring sunny days

If your crafty space is overflowing with all the odds and ends of precious fabrics you can't bear to throw away and know will be perfect for making a patchwork or label at some point, consider storing their loveliness in old kitchen cooking pots or plastic colanders, easily found in charity shops and thrift stores.

crafty ways bring sunny days

polishing
your crafty
soul is
never dull

the everything & anything crochet string bag

Dearest readers,

Now this is a bag you simply must make as there is no end to its uses... Tucked away in a corner of your handbag, it is there for those shopping items you didn't mean to buy but just couldn't resist. At home you can stash your veg, fruit, yarn, fabric scraps, balls of this and that, doily collection and mail. Yes, indeedy, there is no end to its usefulness. Rachelle x

ingredients

* Ball of string, cotton yarn, jute or some other hardwearing sensible thread
* A suitably sized crochet hook for the type of yarn you are using

polishing your crafty soul is never dull

4 chain, join with slip stitch.

3 chain (counts as first stitch), then 8 treble crochet into space, slip stitch to 3 chain – 9 treble crochet.

3 chain (this counts as your first stitch), then 1 treble crochet into first stitch, 2 treble crochet into each space until end, slip stitch to 3 chain – 18 treble crochet.

3 chain and 1 treble crochet into same space (1 treble crochet into next 2 space then 2 treble crochet into next space), repeat to end. Slip stitch to 3 chain.

Repeat last row until the diameter of your base diameter is about 15cm.

5 chain and double crochet into every other stitch for 1 round. Continue 5 chain, double crochet into every stitch space until the bag is the height you want.

To finish, 4 double crochet into every 5 chain space for 1 round.

To make the handle, chain 40 and join with a double crochet into a stitch along the top of the bag, then turn and 40 double crochet into each chain. Secure with a slip stitch into base stitch and break thread.

Join thread with a double crochet onto the opposite side of the bag, making sure there are equal spaces at the sides, and repeat first handle. If you fancy, use some rather lovely fabric string to wrap the handles and make them extra comfy for carrying.

Just a note:

You can even make the bag from plastic string and use it outside to store all your garden bits, collect the eggs from the chickens you may have or a few plastic flowers to bring a dash of colour on those grey days.

Consider blinging your
string bag by wrapping
the handles in frayed
fabric or indeed attaching
a frayed flower or two.

Wearing rose-coloured specs is always a good way to start out. Sometimes they may slip and that is 'a-okay' but at other times they can really show you the way when it comes to seeing potential in secondhand finds. Once you have discovered how wonderful their vision can be, imagine the treasures you'll find.

a 'cluster of doilies' table mat

Dearest readers, I am most fond of a doily or two; for many years they have played a most important part in what I make by hand. For this recipe, it is simply a case of rustling around in your doily stash, pulling out a few of odd size, and spending a happy five minutes stitching them together in a pleasing fashion. You can choose itty-bitty-sized doilies as I have here, or you can chose grand-sized ones to produce a lovely-sized runner to jolly up a dining table or perhaps drape atop a sideboard. Doilies in vintage creams and whites will be sure to look rather fabby, however there are some true granny-coloured ones out there, which when clustered together, I am thinking would make for a splendid runner or table mat. Tif x

ingredients

* doilies
* embroidery thread in happy colours
* embroidery needle
* dress-making pins (optional)

recipe

Take your pile of doilies and lay them out, to see how they fit together in a pleasing fashion. You may have to spend some time swapping them around until all their little edges bump together nicely.

Whilst keeping your doilies in place, start stitching where the doily edges touch together with some coloured embroidery thread. You can do very neat stitching or you can do some random overlapping stitches such as I have, sort of criss crossy style. If you have trouble with your doilies being pesky and shifting around, consider pinning them in place, just to keep them where you want them.

Once all the doilies have been joined to one another, either using the same coloured thread throughout or changing it up a bit, place your table mat on a side table and add some knick knacks to the doily centres. Step back and admire the little cluster, then marvel at how such an easy peasy thing to do can make one's crafty soul feel grand.

If you have more time and more doilies you could consider creating a wonderful tablecloth or indeed the perfect doily throw for over your bed or back of settee.

polishing your crafty soul is never dull

Oh for the love of a doily...

Now, before we begin, the doily is indeed not everyone's cup of tea and for those likers of these lacy delights there are two camps of thought. One is full of like-minded souls who are quite happy to chop, stitch and make new, and the other is horrified at such a notion, preferring to keep their vintage pieces of doily loveliness complete and peachy perfect. We are the ones who like to chop. So now that is cleared up, let us move on with no gasps of horror.

Vintage doilies can be found far and wide and there is often a little basket of them hidden away in a corner of charity shops, secondhand stores, vintage markets, and indeed on the aisles of eBay if you really have no luck elsewhere. Often they will look a bit grey and unloved, be sporting a few holes or tears, but, my dears, none of these treasures should be dismissed. Push those rose-coloured specs way up your nose and hatch a plan. They can be restored to their former glory with a soak in laundry bleach or, failing that, dyed a nice new colour that suits.

A doily to us is the heart of granny chic. There are no boundaries where these little lacy rounds are concerned, and to have them piled high is a sight to see. Oh yes my dears, an essential in one's home, reminding us of what has been before, the history of each and

every one as someone took care and patience to hook each stitch in every lacy circle.

More often than not, these wonders can fix a sticky situation, a sneaky hole, a wonky seam or any manner of terrible deeds and indeed make something as good as new, ready to be proudly displayed around your home.

From lampshades to pillows, stuck on walls, windows and chairs, under bowls of different sizes, from pinny pockets to curtains, there is nothing a doily isn't ready to jump in and help with. Also, if you use a washable paste to attach your doilies, you can remove them at a

later stage and reuse them elsewhere, which we feel is right at the heart of re-using and making do. If you want them to stay put forever, a lick of water-based varnish will do the trick and will also keep them looking good as new.

So once you have decided to give them a new place to rest awhile, they can continue their journey with perhaps another purpose, forging a few new tales to tell.

polishing your crafty soul is never dull

If you find your abode becoming a little too frilly and soft with all the lace and doilies, add a slightly ugly colour or fabric to the mix. Certain shades like mustard, chartreuse, grey and even black can do wonders at giving a little edge to a corner or cluster which has become too sweet.

a dingle dangle door screen

Dearest readers,

There are many wondrous advantages to living on a farm but there is a horror that rears its head in spring and then bothers us all through summer until the weather turns nippy again... the dreaded fly, coming into the house uninvited and making quite a nuisance of itself. But this year I have a plan – one that involves some simple crochet, a few buttons and some rather fetching yarn. *Rachelle x*

ingredients

* a tape measure
* cotton yarn
* suitably sized crochet hook
* buttons, beads, lace bits, fake flowers (and anything else that turns up and would look peachy dangling about)
* 2 or 3 cup hooks

recipe

To begin, measure the width and length of your door and note them down somewhere safe... your handy dandy notebook (see page 138) is a suitable place!

Using your chosen yarn, chain stitch until it is the required length (the width of your door) + 2 chain, turn.

Double crochet into 2nd stitch from the hook and then in each stitch until the end, turn.

2 chain and double crochet into each space. Repeat six times, 8 rows of double crochet in total.

3 chain, skip 1, double crochet into next space, repeat to end, break yarn and sew in threads.

Thread buttons, lace, beads and various what-not onto your cotton yarn, then crochet a string of chain stitches the length of the door, adding in your threaded bits and bobs as you go.

To add in your dingly dangly bits, move each piece up the thread to sit snugly against the hook and then carry on the chain. The button etc. will be trapped between the stitches.

Finish the end of the string with 3–4 buttons to give each thread some weight at the base when it is hung. Repeat to make several strings.

Once you have enough dangly strings, tie them onto the three chain spaces, leaving an empty space between each one.

Attach the horizontal string to the top of your door on several cup hooks and let it dangle.

polishing your crafty soul is never dull

This little gem is indeed a perfect way to use up broken bits of jewellery, old buttons and little scraps from the stash that has been sitting on the shelf just waiting to be loved...

a granny stitched tea cosy

Dearest readers,
No self-respecting granny chic abode would be without a teapot and no teapot should be without a cosy. I personally feel that this is quite essential in the untold wisdom of making the perfect pot of tea. This pattern gives a nod to the all-time granny icon, the crochet blanket, and I think you will agree that when wearing this fine jacket your teapot will indeed brew you the best cup of tea it can.... (Both Tif and I are fans of Yorkshire Tea – just in case you were wondering.) Rachelle x

ingredients

* DK yarn in various shades (I used double knit special by Stylecraft) or any suitable DK scraps that maybe hanging about the place
* 4mm crochet hook

Chain 82 stitches.

In 3rd chain from hook, 2 treble crochet (skip 2, chain 3, treble crochet into next chain) to end. Break thread. 27 treble crochet clusters.

Join yarn with slip stitch in end space of 1st cluster, chain 3, (3 treble crochet in next space), repeat for 12 clusters. Break yarn. Join yarn in next space, chain 3 (counts as 1 treble crochet), 2 treble crochet into same space, (3 treble crochet in next space), repeat to end, 1 treble crochet in end space. Break yarn.

Join yarn with slip stitch in first space, chain 3 (counts as 1 treble crochet), 2 treble crochet into same space, repeat for 12 clusters, 1 treble crochet in end space. Break yarn. Rejoin yarn into 1st space of next treble crochet, chain 3, (3 treble crochet in next space), repeat for 12 clusters.

Repeat rows 3–4 until you have 11 rows in total.

Continue pattern for next row but don't break the yarn at the centre, carry on across the row to join both sides, continue to end.

Repeat as above, but when you get to middle space, 2 treble crochet and then continue.

Join yarn with slip stitch in end space of 1st cluster, chain 3, (3 treble crochet in next space), repeat for 11 treble crochet, 2 treble crochet in next 2 spaces, (3 treble crochet in next space), continue to end, slip stitch into 3rd stitch of chain on the opposite side. Now you have a complete circle.

Join yarn in 1st space, chain 3, 1 treble crochet in same space, (3 treble crochet in next space), repeat, 10 treble crochet, 2 treble crochet in next 3 space, (3 treble crochet in next space), continue to last space, 2 treble crochet. Slip stitch into 3rd stitch of 1st chain.

Join yarn with slip stitch in back space, chain 3, 1 treble crochet, (2 treble crochet in next space, 3 treble crochet in next space), repeat x 5, 2 treble crochet in next space, (2 treble crochet in next space, 3 treble crochet in next space), repeat to last space, 2 treble crochet in last space, slip stitch to chain 3.

Join yarn in space between last 2 treble crochet space of previous row, chain 3, 1 treble crochet. (2 treble crochet in next space) repeat to end. Slip stitch into chain 3.

Join yarn in space between 2 treble crochet directly above handle space, chain 3, 1 treble crochet. In next space 2 treble crochet, then

3 treble crochet in next space, (skip 1 space then 3 treble crochet in next space), repeat to last space, 2 treble crochet, slip stitch to chain 3.

Join yarn, chain 3 (counts as 1 treble crochet), 1 treble crochet, (2 treble crochet in each space), repeat to end, slip stitch to chain 3.

Join yarn, chain 3 (counts as 1 treble crochet), 1 treble crochet into every space to end, slip stitch into chain 3.

Join yarn, chain 3 (counts as 1 treble crochet), 1 treble crochet into every other space, slip stitch into chain 3.

Repeat row 14, break yarn, then thread needle and gather stitches to close the gap…. Sew in all the stragglers and add a pom pom or two – done!

One rule you should always follow when making the best cup of tea in a pot. . . always remove the tea bag after 3-5 minutes. Never ever leave it in, otherwise your second or third cuppa rosie lee will not taste quite right (unless you like it that way of course!).

a travelling tale blanket

Dearest readers,

There is something rather lovely about vintage terry towelling and the patterns and colours it comes in. I have yet to stumble across a terry towelling tablecloth on my thrifty travels, however I have noted you can still find plenty of them on eBay and Etsy in all their kitschy glory. Do not fret if your tablecloth has a few marks or even signs of wear and tear, for this recipe is most suited to using a tablecloth that has seen better days. Every summer, my clan and myself fly across the pond to old Blighty to spend one month travelling around family and friends. We always travel light, as in my head when I am packing, I am imagining warm summer days on the beach and also all the wonderful vintage linens waiting for me to discover upon our travels. Of course, the reality is very few days are warm enough for sitting on the beach. However, the wonder of this little travel blanket is that it is perfectly suited for being wrapped around cold shoulders whilst sitting upon the sand, shivering a little but still intent on eating a 99 ice cream. Tif x

ingredients

* a secondhand terry towelling tablecloth, or some vintage towels stitched together to make a large square or rectangle
* doilies
* snippets of leftover fabrics, selvedges off old bedsheets, ribbons etc.
* embroidery thread
* a special fabric marking pen (or normal pencil will do)
* a trusty sewing machine

polishing your crafty soul is never dull

Wash your tablecloth and run her through the dryer to make sure she is lovely and soft.

Look closely at where there might be the odd stain or a little hole maybe. Taking your stash of doilies, place them over the areas needing a disguise. Pin in place. With your trusty sewing machine and contrasting thread, start in the middle and stitch out to the edge of your doily, stop and turn back towards the centre of the doily, continuing past to the opposite outer edge. Proceed in this fashion, passing through the middle of the doily each time, until you have achieved a 'cartwheel' effect. Like the spokes of a bicycle if you will.

When all your doilies are safely stitched in place, rummage around your stash of ribbons, edgings, and lace. Some may look lovely folded over to make loops, others perfect as they are. Cut into odd-sized lengths and put in a nice handy pile next to your machine. Starting along one edge of the tablecloth, start stitching with your trusty sewing machine, adding a nice

mix of tags and edgings as you go, leaving a little gap in between each one. When you get to the corner, turn your cloth and continue upon your way until all four sides have an eclectic mix of colourful tags.

Now all your edging and doilies are in place, it is time to think about the words you wish to embroider upon your peachy travelling tale blanket. You may wish to think about a journey you once took, or one you will be taking, the places you will visit and things you will see. With a special fabric marking pen, write out the towns, cities or countries along the border of the tablecloth, or you could simply scatter your wording across the whole blanket in a random fashion.

With embroidery thread, backstitch your written word or words with a sharp needle, being careful not to snag the threads in the terry towelling cloth as you stitch. After your wording is complete, run the blanket through the machine again to remove any pen markings and voilà! A travelling tale blanket is ready for journeys and picnics.

Just a note:

It may be you wish to add only one or two places to the blanket for now and, as you travel along with your blanket, packing needle and thread for the journey, you can add to your 'travelling tales' blanket whilst on the go.

a handy dandy fabric jar

Dearest readers,

I appear to be rather addicted to rescuing glass jars from the brink of the recycling bin. When out and about grocery shopping for my clan, I even compare jars and find some are peachier than others. Another place to keep a keen eye out for glass jars if perhaps your larder is not coming up trumps is the thrift store. Once you have a suitable jar (and if necessary, have eaten the contents), give it a nice soak to remove the labels and clean out its inners. Do not fret if some of the glue from the label does not come off, after all you will be covering it with fabric. Righty ho! With that all said, let us begin. Tif x

recipe

With your clean jar all ready to go, figure out how you wish to place the different patterns of your fabric. I tend to cover the bottom two-thirds of the jar in one fabric and the top third in another.

Start at the bottom of your jar, pasting glue on the outside lower edge. Don't go too far up or the glue will start to dry. Put your brush down and carefully press down your first strip. Then add another one where the last one ended. Proceed around the jar in this fashion, building up rows as you go, stopping to add more glue every now and then.

Two thirds of the way up, remember to change your fabric choice if you so wish to. At the top, take the glue over the rim and down inside the jar a tad. With your final strip of fabric at the top, leave enough to fold down over the rim to make a nice-looking edge.

Allow your little jar to dry overnight. In the morning, add glue carefully to the back of your doily or lace scrap and place on the front of your jar. Your handy dandy jar is complete! Add pens, bits and bobs or a few fresh flowers from the yard, sit it in a happy spot and note how handy dandy and pretty it is!

polishing your crafty soul is never dull

Just a note:

I often decide upon buying a particular jam or sauce based on its jar rather than its content. This is perhaps not the best way to go about purchasing your groceries but as I do not do it every trip I tell myself it is 'a-okay' every now and then.

Dearest readers,

It is absolutely essential to have some crocheted blankets of various patterns, colours and styles piled up around the place. This pattern looks quite lovely crocheted in just one colour but it is also ideal for using up all those bits and pieces of yarn left over from other projects and it can easily be done whilst enjoying a Sunday film or travelling on your jollies. Crocheted all in one colour it looks quite tip top with a contrasting colour border around the edges and it is a simple pattern that can be picked up and put down at the drop of a hat. *Rachelle x*

ingredients

* yarns of the same weight in whatever colours take your fancy
* a suitable crochet hook to match your yarn

a granny puff blanket

recipe

Make a chain, counting in multiples of 3 until you reach the required width of your blanket, 2 chain.

3 chain (counts as 1 treble crochet), 2 treble crochet into first chain (skip 2, chain 3, treble crochet into next chain) to end, turn.

3 chain (counts as 1 treble crochet), (puff stitch into next space), 1 chain. Repeat to last 3 treble crochet. 1 treble crochet into end space.

Repeat rows 2–3 until the blanket is the required length.

Puff stitch: Yarn over hook, insert hook into space and pull up a loop, (3 loops on hook), repeat 2 times (7 loops on hook), yarn over hook and pull through all 7 loops on hook, chain 1 to secure. If you would like a puffier stitch, add another loop (9 loops on hook) before crocheting your chain to secure.

a 'hello my name is' banner

Dearest readers, this crocheted banner is perfectly suited to little beings and small critters who take great joy in seeing their name on items. It is easily adapted to a number of other occasions, perhaps a perfect way to say 'happy birthday' or indeed, why not make the caravan in your back yard feel a little loved? This recipe is for an itty bitty size, however just add more stitches and rows and you will have a larger banner, if you so wish. Variations on this recipe which spring to mind: think about leaving some flags without a letter, appliqué a doily upon one or embroider a flower on another. You could even intersperse the crocheted pieces with vintage fabric ones. Yes, I am thinking that would look perfectly peachy indeed. Tif x

ingredients

* leftover yarn from the string bag recipe on page 79 (or any from your stash)
* a suitably sized crochet hook
* a large-eyed needle
* contrasting coloured yarn or thread

recipe (for 1 flag)

Chain 12 (plus 3 for turning).
Row 1: treble crochet to end, chain 3.
Row 2 to 4: repeat row 1.
Row 5: treble crochet to end, chain 2.
Row 6: double crochet to end, break yarn.

This makes one flag.

Repeat to make as many as you require for the word or name you wish to have on the banner. When you have finished all of them, take a needle and sew in all your ends, so everything looks spickety neat.

With your contrasting thread or yarn, embroider the letters upon your flags. You could use basic running stitch, back stitch or chain stitch. Be sure to have the short sides of your flag at the top and bottom before you begin stitching your letters.

Leaving a long tail, chain 10 then slip stitch along the top of your last flag in the word. Then chain 5 and attach your next flag, slip stitching across the top. Continue in this way until you have all your flags attached. Chain 10 and tie off, leaving a long thread. (Be sure to check every now and then your letters are in the correct order.)

And voilà! Hang up the banner so a small being or little critter will feel most loved.

polishing your crafty soul is never dull

Consider making a mini version of
the granny puff blanket on page 106 for your
little critter or small being

a happy wall doily

Dearest readers,

Doilies are one of the building blocks of granny chic style. It is possible to do just as grannies have done for generations, find a nice little sideboard and pop down a doily or two. Then place a forsaken figurine from a charity shop on top and you have yourself the beginnings of a peachy vignette. However, you can also take your doily collection and dabble with it in a multitude of crafty ways, my favourite being to embroider upon their lacy ways odd words or little sayings and pop them on the wall as small reminders. The best sorts of doily to use for embroidering words have a solid linen inner circle. I am especially fond of ones which have coloured stitch work already in place... also, just a thought, this little recipe lends itself nicely to tray cloths too! The sort which has embroidery already done years ago by another crafty soul – how lovely it would be to add your own stitches to its journey through life, and then enjoy it for years to come. Tif x

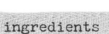

ingredients

* ❉ a doily (cotton centre) or tray cloth
* ❉ a pencil borrowed from a small being in your household
* ❉ embroidery thread in a colour of your choice
* ❉ an embroidery needle

recipe

Ponder which words you wish to stitch. It could be one word like 'home' or 'love'. It could be a name of a small being to place above their bed. If you have room, you may wish to think of a little saying or cheery thought for the day, reminding those who pass by that it is the simple things which matter.

Think about the placement of your word, or words, write them lightly and carefully on the linen with your borrowed pencil. I like to use joined-up handwriting, but you could use all capitals or block letters if preferred. If you make a mistake, do not fret, because you have only pressed lightly with the pencil and you can carefully erase if need be.

Cut a length of your chosen embroidery thread, keeping all six strands together if you wish or splitting them, if you prefer. Thread your needle and start stitching the letters using back stitch, being sure not to pull the stitches too tight. Once the wording is complete, press your doily or cloth with your handy dandy iron, on the reverse side.

Find the perfect place to hang your happy wall doily with a small tack in the wall... I like to hang mine in a cluster with old vintage postcards, little button cards and a magazine tear-out or two. I am also fond of hanging them on their own, so the words and the sentiment behind cannot be missed when walking by.

polishing your crafty soul is never dull

wisdom on yarns

Many folks have many thoughts on which yarns work best for them. For us, living in households of folks and critters, we need our yarny bits of goodness to not only withstand a lot of daily use, but to go through the wash without fear that our handmade lovely will become history. Cost is another factor for many, ourselves included. On occasion we have spent large sums on lovely yarns, spun from natural sources, and indeed, the result is simply peachy, making most treasured items, likely to be handed down the family line. But for practical reasons and for your purse's sake, this is not always possible. So, for that reason, we are most fond of using acrylic blends, cottons and bamboo mixes.

Sometimes you may be lucky and come across a bag or two straight out of a granny's stash and now waiting upon the shelves of despair in your charity shop, but mostly we are thinking you will have to buy new. There are many colours available, but take care, for some simply will not sit well amongst your granny chic colour scheme. However, if you are careful and pick wisely, you will not be disappointed with your final bit of yarny goodness. And just a thought (for on occasion we do have a few)… our biggest tip of all - mix colours with plenty of cream or off white yarns, to avoid overdosing on colour, then you will be most delighted with the results.

polishing your crafty soul is never dull

Crochet and knitted goodness
makes for a lovely mix amongst
the fabrics of a granny chic
home. If you are lacking in
the necessary skills, there are
plenty of places to find such
items handmade by others.
This is a grand way to bring
a handmade feel into your nest
and support handcrafters at
the same time.

polishing your crafty soul is never dull

more crafty
recipes to
fill your
heart with
glee

Please
do not
feed
Stella

Dearest readers,

Now, these chaps are for more than just coats! Painted in the perfect granny colours, covered in a suitably smart crochet jacket, the hanger definitely has a place in your granny chic home. Once you begin your collection, you will quickly find all manner of useful tasks they can perform and a painted hanger can be the basis of oh-so-many variations, from pom poms to lacy bits and bobs. Just let your imagination and materials from your stash run away. *Rachelle x*

spruced up coat hangers

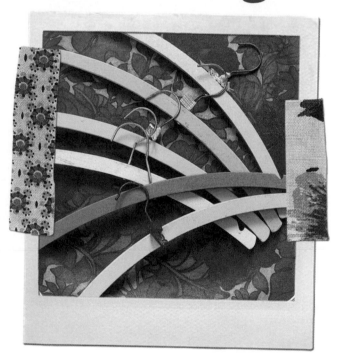

recipe

Lightly sand the hanger and wipe clean. Wrap a piece of masking tape around the base of the hook.

Thinly apply a coat of paint and hang the hanger up to dry.

Repeat the previous step until you are happy with the coverage. Don't be tempted to paint a thick coat as the finish won't be as good.

Once the paint has thoroughly dried, give the hanger a couple of coats of varnish and leave it to dry.

Remove the masking tape and embellish the hanger as you wish.

more crafty recipes to fill your heart with glee

As well as painting your hangers you can indeed wrap them in fabric, using the same method as the chair on page 56. Wrap them in lace or yarn... wallpaper or washi tape, the possibilities are endless.

another terribly wise wisdom

Whilst out and about wandering the aisles of thrifty fine establishments, do not dismiss an item that upon discovery has very little age to it. There is no fine print in the written world of granny chic stating you are not allowed to have modern items within your abode, no sirree! The granny chic home is embracing of all ages. As long as it makes you happy, then trust your granny gut instinct. It might be worth scribbling down in your handy dandy notebook, (the one you made from Rachelle's spiffy recipe on page 138) these three golden granny chic rules.

rule one if your heart pitter patters upon sight, then chances are it is right.

rule two if you hear a chorus of angels sing, you can be sure it is just the thing.

rule three if you feel a tear or two of joy, you've found a treasure for sure, oh boy!

Thus if Mr Doubter pops up upon your shoulder whilst a 'modern secondhand find' is in your hand, you can send him off with a flea in his ear, by reciting the three golden rules.

a 'quirky & jolly' string

Dearest readers,

I am rather fond of garlands, bunting or happy strings around our nest. Call them what you will, at the end of the day they all amount to the same thing, making life and the granny chic home a little jollier. Often I am rather partial to making them from scraps of leftover fabrics, old postcards and book pages, along with any other 'blingy' things which might catch my magpie eye. Oh yes, and the odd kitschy flower is always a winner in my 'garland books'. This simple recipe is a rather organic type of 'happy string', so be sure to place your dingly dangly bits a little randomly and not in an obvious pattern. Before you know it, you will have a 'quirky & jolly' string doing a peachy job of things. *Tif x*

* a crochet hook
* crochet cotton
  (skinny type in any colour
  you may like)
* old book pages
* old postcards
* paper and fabric
  scissors
* odd scraps of lace
  and fabric
* a trusty sewing
  machine
* machine thread
  (in jolly colours)
* kitschy flower heads
  (pulled off the top of their
  stems and on the small side)
* small doilies

recipe

Start by chaining a string with your cotton yarn and hook approximately 120cm long. Hang it up, ready for adding dingly dangly strings as and when you make them. We will call this our 'master string' as it does sound like he knows what he is doing and that he feels very important whilst doing it.

Next, fold and tear narrow strips of your book pages. Do the same for the vintage postcards but do not tear; this time use scissors. Also cut scraps of fabric and lace if you wish to include these in your jolly string.

Gathering up your piles of little strips, take your first few pieces and stitch them together with your trusty sewing machine. Leaving plenty of thread at the top for tying, feed your piece of postcard, book page or fabric under the foot of your machine, leaving a small gap between pieces, then continue stitching until you have several pieces in a row stitched in place. Finish off by leaving long threads.

Continue in this fashion, making some strings longer than others. Tie them onto your master string as and when you complete them. This way you can have an idea of what other pieces you will need to add and whereabouts they will go.

Taking odd flower heads, stitch them in place with needle and thread where you think they look most pleasing.

With hook and cotton yarn, chain a few stitches, slip stitch to the top of a small doily and then continue to chain a further 15 or so stitches. Finish off and tie to your master string. Add baubles or any other pretty itty bitty things you think might work well.

Just a note:

When making this string bear in mind the weight of what you are dingly dangling and also the fact that it is delicate, so best hung out of reach of little inquisitive fingers.

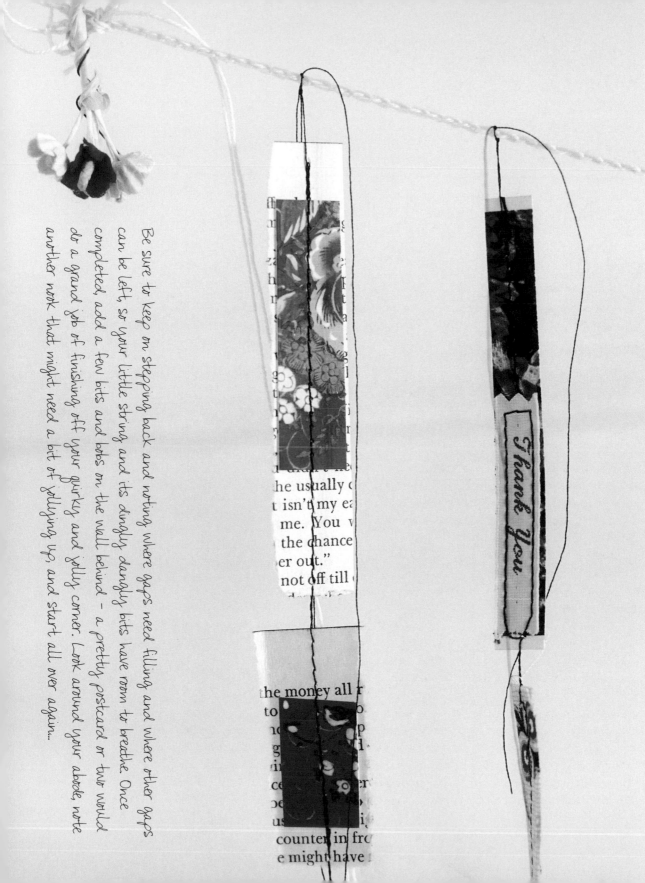

Be sure to keep on stepping back and noting where gaps need filling and where other gaps can be left, so your little string and its dingly danglly bits have room to breathe. Once completed, add a few bits and bobs on the wall behind – a pretty postcard or two would do a grand job of finishing off your quirky and jolly corner. Look around your abode, note another nook that might need a bit of jollying up, and start all over again...

marvellous maude

wisdom on outdoor living

❉ Sometimes it is quite nice, if space permits, to have a little bit of granny chic living outside. Old caravans can still be found for sale at relatively low prices if you are not fussy about the insides. Of course, there are one or two gems with their inners gleaming like the glorious old days to be found, but more often than not their insides have been neglected or worse still removed. Hence a bobby bargain price on their heads.

❉ Find your rose-coloured specs and do not pass up the potential of these sweeties! If their outsides are still in good enough nick, keeping bad weather at bay, there is nothing a granny chic soul cannot put to right on the inside. Consider, if the caravan has some built-ins, whether they are worth saving. It is quite possible that just a lick of paint will make them spickity span once again. If not, then by all means rip them out and start again… trust your crafty soul on this one and the vision you have for your peachy caravan to know what is the best thing to do.

❉ If you are thinking your granny chic caravan will be on the road again, then perhaps you will have to think a little more deeply about making sure everything is fitted, so as not to have it falling all over the place whilst travelling out and about. But if, on the other hand, you see your lovely caravan as a permanent fixture in the back garden, there to be admired in all weathers from the kitchen sink while doing the washing up, well then you do not have to fret in the least about what goes in her, dearest readers, unless it is a passing critter who may be rather partial to a rest on those inviting comfy cushions!

❉ If the floor is a little dodgy, rip it up and go on the hunt for retro inspired flooring. Usually, caravan floors are smallish and odd sized, so look in the discount bargain bin of a flooring store. If one piece isn't large enough, consider two different types of floors and patch them together. Keep your eye open for old hook rugs at the thrift store and charity shops, a nice little scattering underfoot of eclectic floral rugs keeps the old feet warm on a cold morning. Or indeed nice warm sheepskin rugs to bury your toes in as you sip your morning tea.

❉ You could go on the hunt for old caravan curtains or make your own from your vintage stash; doesn't matter if they are mix and match, think florals, think lace and think granny. Once your floor and windows are sorted, think about what you wish to have your little caravan to be. Do you wish others to be able to spend the night in her? Do you wish the children to be able to hole up in her on a rainy summer's afternoon enjoying a board game or playing on their computer games? Or do you wish to keep her all to yourself and make her into a crafting haven… worthy of a ponder? For if a bed is needed then you must make space for this. Look around your home, see what pieces of furniture would lend themselves nicely to a bit of glamping in the back yard, 'granny chic' style. We are quite sure you will be able to rustle up a few willing victims from your collections of furniture and knick knacks around your nest.

✻ Then there is indeed the humble shed to consider if room or desire for a caravan is lacking. It can be a perfect space to paint a peachy colour and stuff full to the brim with all your granny delights, especially if the rest of your household isn't keen on your new found granny ways.

✻ For a more temporary solution and a summer hideout there is always the humble canvas tent. Often found on the aisles of eBay, local advertisement pages and other such places for buying and selling. If you really fancy pushing the boat out there are some rather fancy brand new bell tents or teepee. Again, these can make your granny heart sing with a whole host of blankets, rugs, lacy bits and bobs, the odd stool or two and don't forget some perfectly peachy strings happily dingle dangling in the wind. We highly recommend having an outside granny space to potter in when the sun is high, for it indeed lifts the spirits and makes your heart sing.

…when you are all done, take the weight off your feet in your caravan with a cuppa, and, whilst admiring the view (inside and out), think of a suitable granny name for your lovely new friend, so she may know just how much you truly love her.

General View of Camp Mill Beach, Mididon.

We love our vintage wallpapers! From large retro orange patterns to spriggy vintage itty bitty florals, there is a place for each and every one in our granny chic homes. Now, the trick is to use it sparingly and not go all-out covering every single wall, else we fear you may go a little nutso being surrounded by so much pattern. Indeed, it may even transport you back to the horrors of a 1970s childhood...

If you only have small pieces of wallpaper, then
consider the patchwork effect, lovely for a flat
panelled door or a small wall in a downstairs loo.
Think about covering tops of furniture with a coat of
wallpaper, sealed with varnish to keep it in tippity
top condition. Old wardrobe doors are always the
better for a bit of papering, be it on the inside
or the outside. If you do not care for your kitchen
cupboard doors, think about removing them and lining
the shelves with a fabby vintage pattern. If the
inside of your front door has panels, consider
wallpapering them and adding a chalk board
alongside, using that spiffy chalk board paint
your local paint man sells. Most handy for leaving
messages for the clan and, indeed, words of granny
chic wisdom for yourself.

more crafty recipes to fill your heart with glee

me old china

Sitting down for five minutes with a warmed teapot wearing its fancy jacket, and tea in a cup and saucer is the highlight of our day. A pretty pattern, graceful handle or a heady reminder of summers past at the village fête, where fun, laughter and bunting were accompanied by a brown stewed liquid in a practical but pretty green cup can lift the spirits no end.

Indeed, in times gone by, a wonderful collection of china would have been on display in many a parlour, often in a fancy cabinet and only used for Sunday best... grannies warning us not to venture too close for fear of mischief and sticky fingerprints on their beloved display. Most likely it had all been given as a wedding gift or passed down to the guardians of the next generation.

Sadly, it seems that more often than not these treasures are ending up on the charity shop shelves, but to us they are one of the stalwarts of a granny chic home.

Not just for sipping your morning cuppa from, oh no my dear reader! There are all manner of interesting suggestions for these prized possessions, including the chipped and stained ones, for they too can have a purpose in your abode.

✳ With a few simple supplies even china in the worst state can be rescued. Glue a cup to a saucer, add some gravel and compost and a few suitable plants, and teacup planters are born.

✳ Add some wax, a wick and a florally type scent and, Bob's your uncle, a most perfect centrepiece and the talk of the town, ideal to give to your own granny as a present – she'll be thrilled.

✳ With a nifty ceramic marker, you can scribble a word or two on a plate and hang an inspirational message up high for all to read.

✳ Fill a cup with bird seed and glue to a pole, pop it in the garden and wait patiently for the friendly chirps of the blue tits, they will be very happy feathered friends... Be warned though – if you are owners of free-ranging chickens, there may be general barging of these poles and some birdseed theft.

✳ A perfect way to serve that all-important granny trifle for tea. Make layers of jelly, custard and cream in individual cups, add a few pretty sprinkles, pop on their saucers and serve. If you insist on tradition, add stale sponge cake to the jelly, but we prefer to miss out that step.

So whether you are stacking cups, plates and teapots for a display of the upmost kind, hanging a few plates on the wall to remind you to be thankful each day, or simply sipping that cup of golden goodness, keep your eyes peeled – there is another perfect cup out there waiting for you to give it a forever home...

more crafty recipes to fill your heart with glee

Dearest readers, how many times do you have a bright idea, think of something you need or someone tells you something you simply mustn't forget? Well, this handy dandy notebook is ideal for all those scribbles that simply must be written down. *Rachelle x*

a handy dandy notebook

A super duper way to use up old envelopes, letters and any other used before paper. The more variety within the pages the lovelier it will look.

recipe

Cut or tear strips of paper so they are roughly twice the length of the finished notebook and the finished width you require.

Make your cover in the same way and place it down with the wrong side facing upwards.

Stack your papers (6 or 7 sheets) on top of the cover, lining up all the sides.

Take the top piece of paper and fold it in half, taking care to crease the fold. A back of a spoon is good for this job.

Open the paper back out and lay it on top of the stack. Then, using the clothes peg, clip the pages and the cover together.

Using the fold line as a guide, stitch across the stack on the sewing machine. You can do this by hand, but if so then make some suitable holes with an awl first – far kinder on the fingers!

Fold the layers in half at the stitching and rub the back of a spoon across the crease.

Get scribbling.

vintage decals

We are most partial to a decal or two. They do a jolly good job of cheering things up, but do be careful because it can become highly addictive. You may end up just like Tif who appears to have decaled her whole world and it is only a matter of time before her critters will be sporting them.

You can find lovely vintage decals waiting for you on eBay, or the vintage aisles of Etsy. Occasionally they can be found when rummaging in a vintage mall, estate or car boot sale, but not often. When you do come across them, be sure to check they are in tippity top condition. If you notice a lot of yellowing around the image, it could be they have got damp at some point and the glue has activated. If this is the case they will be no good for transferring. However, sometimes the images are so vintage and pretty, you may consider buying them and just cutting them up and using them as wall art in a cluster pinned up. So best to double check quality before buying. This can be a tricky thing, so it is always a little bit of a risk you take when buying secondhand online.

When getting ready to adhere the decal, follow the instructions and be sure to treat it carefully. Due to their age they can tear easily, so slide them onto the surface with the utmost care and consideration. Once you have decaled one thing,

the need to find another will surely follow. We have found many willing victims in our own granny chic nests and on these pages you will see a few of those 'happy to be decaled' victims to inspire you to look around and see who might be a good volunteer in your own home.

Of course, if you have no luck in finding vintage decals, do not fret for it is possible to make your own! All you need is a camera, a printer, spray varnish and a sheet of clear-backed decal paper, which can be found online or at your local craft supply store. Armed with your supplies, look at your vintage china collection and find one with a floral pattern you like. Take a close-up photo and upload it to your computer. Crop in as close as you can and reading the instructions that come with your decal paper, print off the correct size to fit your willing 'to be decaled' victim. Spray your printed decal paper with several coats of

varnish, allowing drying time in between. (Do read the instructions for your decal paper. They may not be the same as ours and we would not wish you to be disappointed by the outcome).

Once your picture is dry, carefully cut around it as close as you can to the floral shape. This can be a bit fiddly, so use tiny pointed scissors if need be or perhaps a craft knife. We also find nail scissors can get the job done quite nicely too. Once again following the directions, soak your picture in warm water for a few seconds and then carefully slide it into place. Pat your applied decal carefully dry with a cloth to avoid air bubbles and slipping out of place. Step back, wait patiently for the decal to dry and, whilst doing so, admire the fact you have made your own vintage-inspired decal and cheered up a willing furniture victim in your home who felt a little sad.

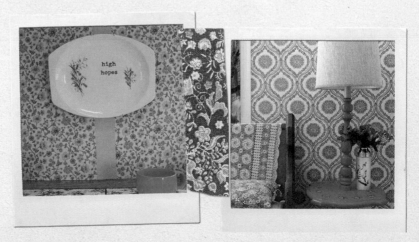

more crafty recipes to fill your heart with glee

After a bit of shuffling around your granny abode to
fit in your lovely new painted peach, sit back and
admire your handy work and marvel at its charming
painted ways with decals of delightfulness.

a peachy painted shelf of decal delightfulness

Dearest readers,

at the heart of every granny chic abode is a mis-matched collection of furniture, wooden pieces of a bygone era with a story to tell, often looking a little the worse for wear. However, despite their outward state, they have solid bones, a good soul, and with a few simple steps it is possible to transform their weary ways so they are once again resplendent. Tif x

ingredients

* a lost, but found again piece of furniture (a small table, a chair or a magazine rack – whatever your thrifty eye has caught when pottling for a forsaken treasure. For the purpose of this recipe I have used a shelf)
* sandpaper (medium grit should be perfectly good)
* good-quality paintbrush (important for getting a nice finish)
* undercoat paint
* good-quality top coat paint
* vintage decals

recipe

Give the shelf a good sand, being sure to follow the grain of the wood rather than going against it. If the shelf has an existing thick coat of glossy varnish you will have to make sure you do a good job so your paint has something to adhere to. If it's too glossy, your paint won't be happy.

Wipe off any dust and brush an undercoat all over. If the piece is of dark wood or with a dark stain, I suggest you choose an undercoat with a stain block built in. Read the side of the paint tin or ask the advice of your local paint man. He is always full of wise words when it comes to what paints do which job best.

When your undercoat is all dry, you can begin with the top coats. It is best to do several thinner top coats rather than one thick coat and have drips appearing all over the place. Work methodically, brushing in the same direction. Check for drips before placing your paintbrush in a sealed bag and popping it in the refrigerator to keep it from drying out. When the shelf is dry to the touch, do the next coat. Continue in this way until the desired coverage is achieved. Wash your brush thoroughly, hang it to dry, and store your paint carefully for using another time.

Place the shelf somewhere safe to cure (dry thoroughly). This may take a few days. Once your newly-painted furniture has had time to adjust to its new coat, take some vintage decals, ponder their placement and then go about 'decaling' your lovely found treasure.

more crafty recipes to fill your heart with glee

wisdom on painted furniture

❋ When debating which furniture you may care to bring home, think solid well-made lines like mid-century or farmhouse pieces to balance out all the lace and doilies. If a need for pine wood is a must, as that is what you have, and it is of the new pine variety, then consider painting it a lovely colour to give a new piece of wood an aged charm. On the other hand, old pine pieces are fetching just as they are and can lend warmth to the home if there is a lot of white, so consider carefully before painting.

❋ Your painted furniture will only be as good as the prep you put in — très dull we know. But you must at least give a little key to the piece with a once-over using sandpaper. Key is a very spiffy term used by those in the know for creating a scuffed surface to an area you are wishing to paint, usually with the aid of sandpaper, thus losing some of the gloss on the original surface and giving the new coat of paint something to grip to as it dries.

❋ If painting with colours is a little scary, do it in little steps. Consider a collection of old frames all painted in the same tone. Or go for one big framed picture and paint it a bright jolly colour to pop on a white wall. If you decide it is not for you, it won't take five minutes to change it back to a more neutral colour. If the pop of colour cheers you up, branch out and go for a side table or little drawer unit and brighten that up too.

It is very well advised to befriend your local paint-mixing chaps as they will be able to mix all manner of granny colours. Ours are most clever and can match almost any shade from even the smallest of scraps or samples. So do not despair if you cannot find the perfect colour since there is always help at hand.

more crafty recipes to fill your heart with glee

✳ Truly our experiences have taught us that nothing stands the test of time and gives a peachy perfect finish quite like a quality paint. If you are new to the notion of painting your furniture, a good undercoat is worth the time to stop the underneath seeping through. And always do your brushstrokes in the same direction, following the grain of the wood.

✲ Do not be afraid of kitschy items you come across on your travels. The right balance adds a lovely mix to your granny chic abode. After all, grannies are not afraid of the odd kitsch figurine and neither should you be.

wisdom on collecting

✲ Collecting odds and ends of china whenever you come across them will make for a splendidly laid table. The granny chic home never lays a table all matchy matchy but embraces the eclectic vibe that comes from a table adorned with a mish mash of patterns and colours.

✲ Collections, be they china, fabric, doilies or chairs, all play a most important part in granny chic living and are perfectly healthy. Consider how you display them, keeping them nice and tidy and with plenty of space for their peachiness to breath and shine.

more crafty recipes to fill your heart with glee

suitcases
inspiration

Old vintage suitcases can still be found relatively easily at charity shops, thrift stores and rummage sales. They range from the very old sort, more box-like in shape, with leather trim detailing, to the more recent retro-styled ones that come in the most marvellous granny chic colours of mustard, teal, grolly green and peachy pink. Sometimes it's hard to think what you might do with such a thing when stumbling across it out and about browsing the shelves of despair, but if you ever find one in peachy perfect condition, snap it up, for there are many uses for this fine example of a bygone era and the wonder of its aesthetics for even everyday things.

Simple uses could be for storage under the bed, perhaps a yarn stash needs to be hoarded or magazines contained. Nice to keep collections all spickity span from dust, stored away, and how lovely to see vintage handles peeking out from beneath a bed and its many layers of vintage linens and handmade blankets.

Stacked high atop a cupboard or closet is always a pleasing way to display your collection of suitcases, once again a perfect place to store bits and bobs. If perhaps you are forgetful in your ways, a lovely addition would be to hand-make luggage labels depicting in words or pictures what may be found inside each suitcase.

If your suitcases are of the flat-sided sort, they may do a rather grand job of stacking up nicely to make a side table. Most handy near the settee or perhaps next to the bed, think about the handles and whether they could do with a bit of feeling loved. Crochet them little covers or indeed wrap them, using your handy dandy fabric yarn balls (you can find out how make these delightful objects on page 61).

Perhaps your found suitcase is a little weary from years of travelling. Do not despair, for as long as its bones are good, there is still plenty of life left for it to give. Consider covering up the front and back panels with fabric or wallpaper. Or perhaps create a collage mish-mash of images, postcards and tear-outs which make you happy...stuck down in a random fashion they may add a little 'jolly-ness' to its scuffed-up exterior and make for the perfect travel companion when out and about.

Little critters can be most fond of sleeping in suitcases. You can remove the lid if you wish or prevent it from closing by screwing a block of wood at the back of the suitcase on the outside. Thus making it safe for little critters to curl up in without fear, not to mention 'health and safety' would be most happy with the results of your thoughtful ways.

Vintage suitcases can also make for handy dandy shelving. Remove the lid and consider whether the inners are a little worse for wear, covering with a patchwork of fabric, using glue which is good at sticking material together, if they are. Use two hefty screws to attach the case to the wall so it does not tumble down, and place a lovely stack of vintage linens inside for others to admire. This might look rather lovely with several different suitcase shelves in a row, each doing a grand job of looking perfectly granny chic whilst holding doilies, lace, table runners and fabrics... most handy dandy indeed!

more crafty recipes to fill your heart with glee

wisdom on fake flowers

Do not dismiss fake flowers for springifying your nest. Sometimes, when you have lovely critters like free-ranging hens, it can be rather tricky to amass borders full of blooms unless you clearly stake out a little spot for them to grow. An alternative would be to see what marvels are available in the faux flower aisle. We are not talking dried flowers covered in dust, more your kitschy silk flowers in wonderful granny chic colours. Granny knicker peachy pink is by far the most treasured to come across.

more crafty recipes to fill your heart with glee

ever useful snippets

An absolute must in all granny chic homes is a little box of handy dandy things. This is a box that can come to your rescue in the stickiest of situations. Things it must contain include a hammer, pliers, staple gun and staples, various scissors, paper and fabric, craft knife blades, glue, masking tape, odd screws and nails, a roll of small plastic bags and anything else you may need at any given moment. This is also a good place to store an extra sewing kit, as you never know when or where there will be a need for a needle and thread.

wisdom
on what-not

Now, there is always a place
for various what-not in a granny
chic home, consisting of all
the bits and bobs you may
indeed need one day, though you
don't know when. There are many
doubters out there who would
hurriedly point the finger and
exclaim that you are hoarding
junk, but this is not the case.
You must be wary, though, that
your stash does not get out of
hand and grow into piles around
your home, and you must be
inventive about how you display
these treasures. Jars full of
bits, labelled with their
contents, can make a peachy
sight on a shelf above a
doorway. Old shopping baskets
full of lacy pieces and scraps,
ideal to trim all sorts of
projects. A big sweetie jar full
of tape measures (believe me,
you can never have enough of
those!). Plastic colanders, old
pans or china serving tureens
filled to bursting with balls
of scrap fabric yarn or the
leftovers of your crochet
project. The possibilities are
endless, dearest readers, and
your hoard can indeed become a
treasured part of the décor,
filling you with joy each time
you catch a glimpse from the
corner of your eye.

more crafty recipes to fill your heart with glee

dottie angel

LITTLE BOX OF

ALWAYS HOLD YOUR HEAD
UP HIGH.
IT KEEPS YOU FROM
STEPPING ON YOUR EARS!

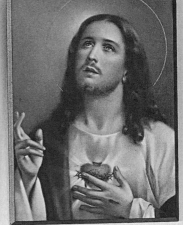

NEW HOME,
SWEET HOME

dottie angel

Luckyday

terribly
interesting
things for
your crafty
soul to
know

handy hints on channelling your inner crafty granny chic soul

Not only do our homes reflect our deep-rooted love for the heritage and creativity handed down by grannies of bygone eras, but our daily attire does too. If perhaps you have found it a little tricky to discover your inner granny soul and are struggling to keep those rose-coloured specs firmly pushed up your nose and this in turn is making your crafting more pants than peachy perfect, then read on.

rose-coloured specs

We have mentioned rose-coloured specs are most important when out and about looking for potential in secondhand finds. However, it may also be quite true to say, when home and dabbling in some handcraftedness, you perhaps require a little visual aid in the way of glasses. Do not despair at the thought of wearing spectacles, for indeed, these are the perfect accompaniment to the granny chic ensemble. May we suggest you find a rather nice pair with a lovely vintage-inspired frame, perhaps in tortoiseshell or indeed, black? Another thought would be to keep your beady eye out for an old original frame on your thrifty travels and consider having a prescription lens put in them.

clogs

Wearing clogs upon your feet and clippity-clopping around the home can be a most satisfactory thing to do. If your floors are without carpet, the sound will give others the impression you are doing things of the utmost importance and they will be none the wiser to the fact that you are only shuffling one knick knack or piece of furniture from one room to the other. When striding around in clogs, a feeling of accomplishment and authority within your creative moments is always achieved and you are left feeling, at the end of the day, that your hours have been well spent and without a doubt, the next day is bound to be filled with more crafty making moments.

pinny

A pinny is a must for everyday attire. Whether you like a half or a whole, they are not only most-sensible attire, saving your frock from blobs of what-not during the day, but they are also an excuse to layer a number of vintage patterns and colours whilst being practical to boot. If perhaps you are not convinced, trying wearing a half pinny wrapped around a skirt of vintage florals, add in your clogs, pop on your granny specs (rose-coloured or real) and wear for one whole day. We guarantee you will find that not only are you prepared for all eventualities (especially when requiring a handy pocket for your vintage hanky and any number of miscellanies your day brings with it), but you will feel most peachy perfect. Before you know it, your granny chic crafty soul will be channelled and raring to go.

terribly interesting things for your crafty soul to know

crochet terms translated

In this book all recipes have been written using UK crochet terms, but we are well aware there are many folks who are familiar with the USA terms, Tif included! So to help you with figuring out the patterns, whatever terms you have learnt, below you will find a handy dandy chart to aid you on your crafty way…

UK	US
double crochet	single crochet
half treble crochet	half double crochet
treble crochet	double crochet
double treble crochet	treble crochet

wisdom on learning to crochet

✳ In this book, the recipes do require you already know how to crochet. If you do not know how, or indeed are very shiny new at doing so, do not fret or hang your head and weep. For there is plenty of help out there to get you started and before you know, you will be just like us, addicted to a bit of daily twiddling with yarn and hook. Rachelle has been dabbling with crochet forever and a day; however Tif is a 'found it later in life' crocheter, so do not give up hope, just keep on trying and one day, an 'ah ha' moment of the utmost kind will happen. You can go online and find many video tutorial sources to show you how to get started, and we do highly recommend a visual learning process; somehow it is easier to be shown than to read it. However, we really truly think the best way to learn a new craft such as crocheting is to get out and about in your local community and find classes being held.

✳ The past few years have seen a resurgence in folks wishing to learn the crafts their grannies knew, and the demand has led to wonderful quirky stores opening up on the high street. They stock yarn, fabrics and threads alongside running lovely workshops for crafty souls to learn a thing or two. Before you know it, you will not only be a dab hand at crocheting (or another craft), but you will also have a wonderful venue to meet up with other like-minded crafty types and spend your time wisely. If this indeed is not an option and there are no workshops nearby, then get together with a few friends and have a go at learning with each other, or persuade a wise soul to come along and teach you. Many a pleasant afternoon can be spent with tea, cake, yarn and a few friends, absolutely crafting for the soul.

terribly interesting things for your crafty soul to know

'we don't see things as they are
we see them as we are' Anais Nin

The beauty of granny chic style is that it can cost very little and you can become most canny at finding a right bobby bargain. However, you can also look around your nest and see what is ripe for a freshen-up. Some things you have already 'granny chic-ed' before are perhaps looking for a little new coat. Often you can find what you are looking for just by having a rootle around the house and re-using things in another room in another way.

If indeed there comes
a time when one of your
treasures is beyond
saving, patching,
gluing, sticking or
stitching, before you
cast it aside pull it
apart and remove anything
that might be of use
elsewhere. Save buttons
and zips from clothes.
Broken and cracked china
does a peachy job in the
garden. Knobs from
cupboards, even old
screws all have a place
in a granny chic stash.

crafty ways bring sunny days

It is perfectly acceptable to have a cupboard of crafty sins and faux pas. Both of us when working on a piece have at some point come a cropper, however instead of throwing the 'offending item' in the bin, we put it in our 'cupboard of crafty sins' and go about our merry way without a backward glance. Sometime later, when the mood strikes you have several options to consider. Option one, retrieve your faux pas, fix it up and finish it off, wondering all along why you lost faith in your abilities. Or there is option two. If it truly is beyond repair or rescue, then snippity snip it up, reuse and recycle in some other peachy way so as not to waste your precious materials.

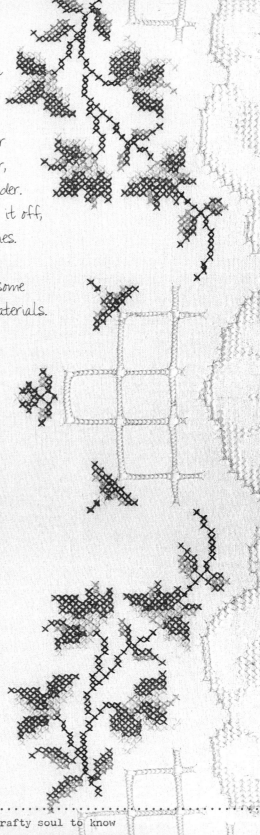

terribly interesting things for your crafty soul to know

resources

UK

****

charity shops

There are many worthy charity stores in the UK, supporting all manner of excellent causes and they are indeed fine places to purchase many bits and bobs. In no time at all, you will come to have your favourites and be able to browse along the shelves and discover treasures to add to your home. Some are filled with lovely volunteers who will greet you with a cheery smile and after frequent visits will even go out of their way to rummage around in the back to find just the thing you are looking for.

Age UK (formerly known as Age Concern and Help the Aged) runs excellent shops around the UK. The South Lakes Warehouse is especially peachy, and visits are made so much easier with the aid of Ann and her biscuit stash, which keeps small beings quiet whilst you wander the aisles searching for treasure.
www.ageuk.org.uk

We have great respect for the charity, Emmaus, and all that it stands for, and it quite frankly always has something to offer for the granny chic home.
www.emmaus.org.uk

online sites for secondhand goodness

Freegle is a fantastic resource for finding some perfect furniture for your granny chic home, preventing the crime of sending it to the tip. Wonderful people pass on great stuff, often with a tale to tell. For us, this is the perfect way to fill your house with amazing furniture and give it a new lease of life. And don't forget to pass on your bits and bobs so that they can continue their journey elsewhere.
www.freegle.org.uk

eBay
For those of us who live in the back of beyond, far from charity shops and who enjoy a regular browse of granny goodness there is always treasure to be found on eBay. Plus there's nothing

like receiving a parcel of goodies in the post, I think you will quite agree. Note down the names and styles of things you like and add them to a saved search so you never miss out on a sneaky listing of just the item you were looking for.
www.ebay.co.uk

good source of yarn, patterns and advice

Knit Rowan is an excellent UK resource for all things yarn, from patterns to advice, plus where to buy the most peachiest of yarn.
www.knitrowan.com

USA

****

thrift stores

There are many fabby thrift stores in the US and they tend to be large and contain more shelves of despair than we ever see in the UK. If you are a regular, and are patient enough to trawl through the crappity crap, it is possible to find practically everything the granny chic abode requires. Look online to

track down your nearest thrift store or think about finding one that supports a charity close to your heart.
www.goodwill.org
www.valuevillage.com

online sites for secondhand goodness

Sometimes it is not possible to get out and about for a bit of secondhand pottling. If this is the case, it is perfectly acceptable behaviour to spend a few quality moments 'window shopping' the aisles of online secondhand sites such as Etsy, eBay or Craigslist.
www.etsy.com
www.ebay.com
www.craigslist.org

good source of yarn, patterns and advice

There are many sites online which have a multitude of patterns and advice offered for free. These are relatively easy to stumble across just by doing a simple search on your computer. However, we do think Lion Brand is pretty peachy for patterns, many of which have a granny chic charm about them. Do not dismiss a pattern because you think the colours are not to your liking. It is the style of the item you should be looking at, so pop on your rose-coloured specs and then choose a perfect granny colour to make it into something more suited to your home. www.lionbrand.com

Australia
****
Here are some peachy places you may care to know, kindly provided by our crafty buddy Pip Lincolne who knows a thing or two about Granny Chic! You can find out more about Pip and her crafty granny ways by visiting her here: www.meetmeatmikes.com

vintage shopping
Sydney:
Rozelle Markets www.rozellemarkets.com.au
Melbourne:
Camberwell Market
Lost and Found Market
www.lostandfound-market.com.au
The Mill Markets
www.millmarkets.com.au
Vintage Shed Tyabb
www.thevintageshed.com.au
and online at Etsy & eBay
www.ebay.com.au
www.etsy.com

charity shopping
Savers Outlets
www.savers.com.au
The Salvation Army
www.salvationarmy.org.au
Vinnies
www.vinnies.org.au
Smaller op-shops (Animal Aid and RSPCA)
www.animalaid.com.au
www.rspca.com.au

fabric shopping
Patchwork on Central Park
www.patchworkoncentralpark.com.au
Ink & Spindle
www.inkandspindle.com.au
Calico and Ivy
www.calicoandivy.com.au
Kelani Fabric
www.kelanifabric.com.au
Spotlight
www.spotlight.com.au

yarn
Bendigo Woollen Mills
www.bendigowoollen-mills.com.au
The Wool Shack
www.thewoolshack.com
Yarn Barn
www.yarnbarn.com.au

paint shop
Porters (Fitzroy, Melbourne)
www.porterspaints.com

Do not fret if your first efforts are more pants than peachy and you feel your crafty soul sink lower and lower into your clogs. All is not lost! Walk away, make a cuppa, 'pottle and ponder', even shuffle around a thing or two... then return to the scene of the crafty crime with fresh eyes and high hopes. Maybe not the same day, or even the same week, but chances are upon return you will see things are way more peachy than originally thought and not the least bit pants.

suppliers

UK

****

yarn

Stylecraft are a most excellent supplier of acrylic yarn at prices most pockets can afford. The yarns wash well and are easy to work with. The yarn comes in a super range of colours and are especially suited to a house where a wool allergy resides. www.stylecraft-yarns. co.uk

paint

Farrow & Ball are one of the best paints we have found to use, especially on an older property. Their emulsions and colour range suit those houses sporting crumbly walls and damp patches rather well. They also have a most spiffy range of grey shades. www.farrow-ball.com

It is also an absolute must to become a regular visitor at your local paint mix shop, where the wonderful staff will understand your strange paint requests. If you wave a photograph under their noses, or show them a particular shade on a charity shop find, or even bring along a paint scraping, you may find that they can work their magic with their fabby machine and mix up the perfect paint. If you are ever in the Yorkshire Dales area, be sure to visit the lovely ladies at Ashfield DIY in Settle. They are paint-mixing geniuses and have bags of patience for those with a granny chic soul. Ashfield DIY in Settle Station Road, Town Centre, Settle BD24 9AA 01729 823 002

fabric

There is a fabric that we both covet considerably. Not only is it a joy to stitch, but each and every ditsy print or marvellous colour combination is a delight to our eyes. It is the one and only Liberty Tana Lawn and indeed every granny chic home should have some. www.liberty.co.uk

Now, in exactly the same way you build relationships by being loyal to your local paint shop, so you should nurture one with the local fabric establishment. For they will be your staples in your crafty world. One of our favourites is a little factory shop in Lancaster, UK called Standfast & Barracks. They have the loveliest of staff and Jack, the manager, has quite a twinkle in his eye. The staff will always go out of their way to find you the perfect fabric. To be perfectly honest, it's worth making a special trip to visit, but be sure to take a full purse. www.standfast-barracks. com

hanging lamp cord kits and bark cloth goodness

If perhaps upon seeing the recipe for making a patched and pieced hanging lampshade you are inspired to give it a whirl, may we recommend the home of Folly & Glee for finding the perfect flex kit for hanging your sweetie for all to admire? Not only do Folly & Glee provide a wealth of colours and fixings to choose from, but they also make the most marvellous barkcloth lampshades, made in the UK and perfectly suited to hang with pride in any granny chic home. www.follyandglee.co.uk

USA

****

yarn

We are most fond of yarn by Lion Brand since it washes brilliantly and comes in perfectly peachy colours. If you are not fond of acrylic mix yarns, we beg you to think again... Give a few of theirs a try and then we are quite sure, in no time at all, you will become 'a believer'. www.lionbrand.com

paint

We are particular about our paints, as you may have noted in this book! Stateside, there are many on offer at your local hardware store, where things can be custom colour matched. However nothing appears to be quite so spiffy as Benjamin Moore Aura paint. Indoors or outdoors, it just keeps on doing the job it is supposed to do, surviving daily household knocks brilliantly and with little complaint. Your local paint man will always be willing to mix any colour in the Aura range, and you do not have to pick only Aura's colour palette. Make friends with your paint man. You will be amazed how after a little while they no longer roll their eyes at your odd requests when dragging in an item to be colour matched, but rather smile happily and think how charming you are (if slightly eccentric) – someone to brighten up their day amongst the usual mixing of boring beige shades. www.benjaminmoore. com

clogs we are fond of wearing

We do love our clogs! Be they boots, clogs or sandals, we do like to spend our day wisely in them, clippity clopping around. We may be just doing our daily chores of sorting out our critters and clan, or perhaps we are crafting or pottling, either way, we feel most happy with clogs on our feet. There are many clog makers in the world but here are a few that we think are the bees' knees. Indeed, more often than not, they are the makers of the clogs we wear daily on our feet.
Troentorp clogs www. onlineclogstore.com
Lotta clogs www.lotta-fromstockholm.co.uk
Bjorn Clogs www.bjorn-clogs.co.uk
Sanita Clogs www.sanita-footwear.com

wallpaper places worth a gander

Vintage and retro wallpapers are at the heart of the granny chic home. You may be lucky enough to come across one or two rolls tucked in the corner of your local charity shop, but it is getting harder and harder to discover such treasure on thrifty jollies. Here are a few places we have found online which have a peachy selection.
Johnny-Tapete www. vintage-wallpaper.com (fabby selection and they are willing to ship worldwide)
Graham and brown www. grahambrown.com (not old but has some lovely prints most suited to a granny chic home)
Vintage wallpapers www. vintagewallpapers.be

perfectly peachy vintage fabrics

Donna Flower is a treasure trove of online fabric finds, beautifully curated by Donna herself, and she certainly knows a thing or two about vintage fabrics. If perchance you are looking for a large selection all under one roof, this would be the place to go 'online browsing'. Donna is always on hand to answer your questions and search out even the most unlikely pieces of fabric goodness.
www.donnaflower.com

thanking you kindly

Judith, Sandy, Helen and Cath, many thanks indeed for rustling around your kitchen drawers to locate your rose-coloured specs, embracing all that we offered up as wisdom on granny chic style, and giving it a grand home in the pages of this book. You are the bees' knees to us!

Tif

Thanks must go to my granny Vera and my grandmother Jane for showing me from an early age how to feel a little crafty with knitting needles and sewing ways. Unbeknownst to me at the time, just seeing you wisely spend moments hand-making gave me a lifetime of appreciation for grannies around the globe and the goodness that comes from their crafty making hands.

To my mother Gill, whom I watched as a young child, pottling happily around our family nest, making curtains, painting and papering walls and teaching me just by sight how one goes about making a house into a home. I have no doubt the need so deep inside of me to continually do the same for my own home, came from seeing your incredible energy and enjoyment of 'keeping house' with your own hands and secondhand finds.

My crafty book writing buddy Rachelle! Gosh, how blessed I was by the handcrafted secondhand gods when they aligned our paths. I would not, could not, have gone through this process with another, for you have been my friend, my therapist and my crafty soul 'granny chic' twin and for that, I am thanking you kindly.

Hurrah hooray for my adopted auntie Vickie, who kept me sane along the way with her tea and friendship... without which I would surely have stumbled.

To my Man and my clan, thank you for living amongst my doilified world without complaint! Without you and your understanding ways for my need to 'granny chic' our home, this book would never have come about... I have no doubt.

Rachelle

Thank you my dearest nana Beatty, a granny whose endless patience taught me to knit, gave me my first sewing machine and the love of a good tabard pinny. You were my rock and I still miss you very much.

Thanks to the inspirational Ted and Agnes for their crazy hoarding ways, their collections of wonders from Ted's globetrotting, and their lifelong love of all things china.

Thank you to my grumpy, cantankerous Dad, Michael, who dragged me around boot fairs, DIY shops, junk yards, and even had me clambering over cars at the scrap merchant. I always had free range with his tools, since, as he would tell me on many an occasion, 'if you never have a go you'll never learn'.

A huge thank you to my book writing pal Tif, who inspires me on a daily basis, and makes me laugh out loud and realise that I am not alone in the way I see the world. We had what seemed an impossible timescale to write this book in, not to mention the time difference and various crazy ideas that have side-tracked us, but the project has brought out our strengths when working together, and built a friendship to last.

Thank you to my little sister, who has tried and tested the crochet patterns for me and all the left-handed folk out there. I am so glad she has finally found her crafty soul, for indeed it is starting to shine and be sure not to listen to Mr Doubter for he will do you no good.

And lastly for my husband Keith and my doubting children, with their rolling eyes and quiet sighs. Putting up with my constant shifting, painting, stitching and changing the house around, for fetching and carrying and surviving the mammoth rows half way up the stairs whilst balancing yet another chest of drawers. Without you all my world wouldn't be half as rosy.

terribly interesting things for your crafty soul to know